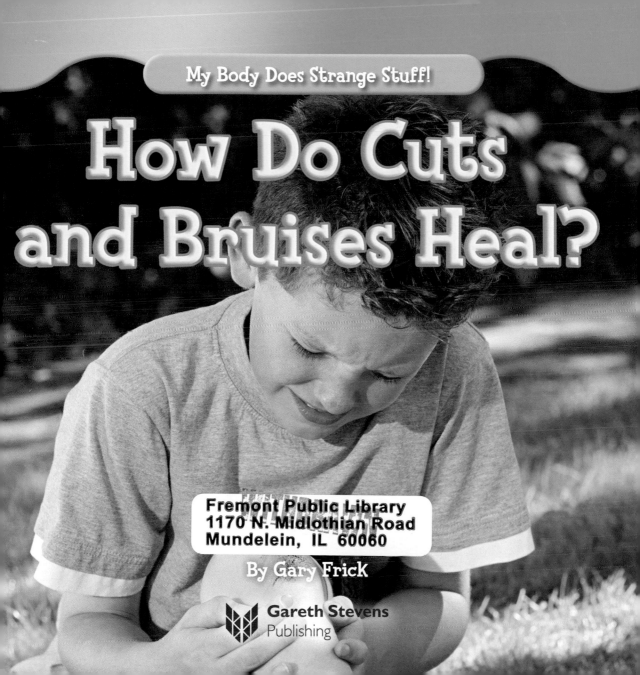

My Body Does Strange Stuff!

How Do Cuts and Bruises Heal?

By Gary Frick

Gareth Stevens
Publishing

Please visit our website, www.garethstevens.com. For a free color catalog of all our high-quality books, call toll free 1-800-542-2595 or fax 1-877-542-2596.

Library of Congress Cataloging-in-Publication Data

Frick, Gary.
How do cuts and bruises heal? / by Gary Frick.
  p. cm. — (My body does strange stuff)
Includes index.
ISBN 978-1-4824-0241-4 (pbk.)
ISBN 978-1-4824-0242-1 (6-pack)
ISBN 978-1-4824-0234-6 (library binding)
1. Wound healing — Juvenile literature. 2. Wounds and injuries — Juvenile literature. 3. Bruises — Juvenile literature. I. Title.
RD93.F75 2014
612—dc23

Published in 2014 by
Gareth Stevens Publishing
111 East 14th Street, Suite 349
New York, NY 10003

Designer: Michael J. Flynn
Editor: Greg Roza

Photo credits: Cover, pp. 1, 5, 21 Image Source/Getty Images; p. 7 (bruise) Edward Kinsman/Photo Researchers/Getty Images; p. 7 (cut) FCG/Shutterstock.com; p. 9 Melianiaka Kanstantsin/Shutterstock.com; p. 11 Suzanne Tucker/Getty Images; p. 13 (scraped arm) Katrina Brown/Shutterstock.com; p. 13 (white blood cell) Cultura Science/Rolf Ritter/Oxford Science/Getty Images; p. 14 2xSamara.com/Shutterstock.com; p. 17 Izf/Shutterstock.com; p. 19 Lukiyanova Natalia/frenta/Getty Images.

Printed in the United States of America

CPSIA compliance information: Batch #CW14GS: For further information contact Gareth Stevens, New York, New York at 1-800-542-2595.

Contents

Boldface words appear in the glossary.

Ouch!

Cuts and bruises happen to everyone. You may cut your hand while riding your bike. You may bump into a table in a dark room and bruise (BROOZ) your knee. Luckily for you, your body knows how to heal cuts and bruises!

5

Safe Inside Your Skin

Our skin is very important. It keeps **germs** out of our bodies and keeps our insides safe. However, sometimes our skin can be injured, or hurt. Something sharp can cut skin. A fall or hit can bruise skin.

cut

bruise

It's in My Blood!

What's the first thing you notice after getting cut? Blood! Blood carries cells that heal cuts. Platelets are cells that stick together. They gather at a cut and form a **clot**. This stops more blood from leaking out of you.

9

Clots harden and form scabs. Scabs keep germs out of the body. Once the skin is done healing, the scab falls off by itself. Never pick at a scab. The cut can bleed again, and a **scar** may form.

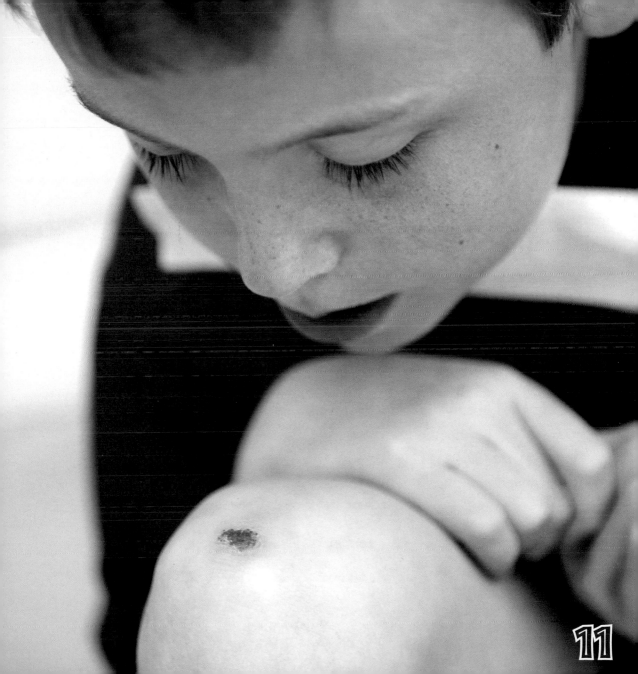

Blood also carries white blood cells. When you get a cut, white blood cells rush to the **wound**. They find and kill germs that try to get into your body. This helps you stay healthy.

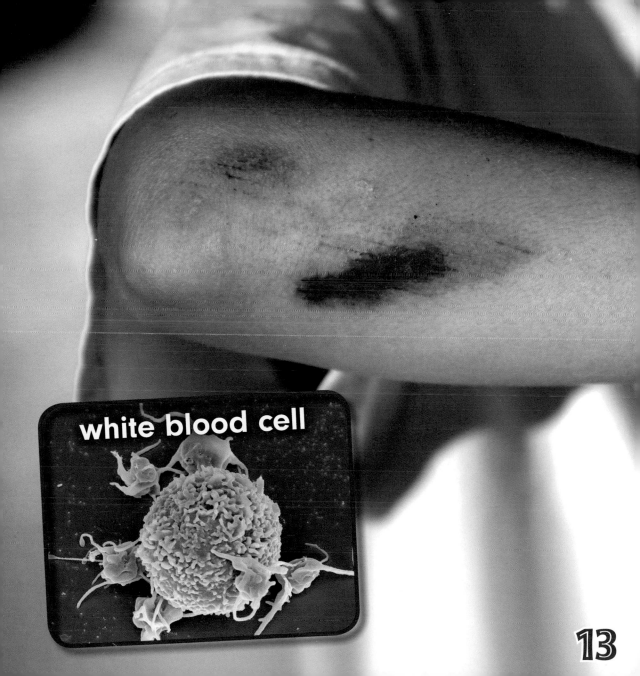

white blood cell

13

Caring for Cuts

If you get a cut, press a clean cloth against it to stop the bleeding. Keep the cut clean and covered to avoid germs. A doctor may need to give you **stitches** if the cut is deep or long, or if it won't stop bleeding.

HOW CUTS HEAL

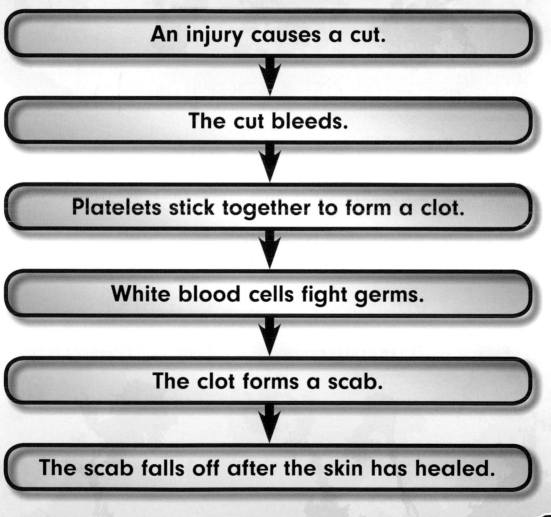

An injury causes a cut.

The cut bleeds.

Platelets stick together to form a clot.

White blood cells fight germs.

The clot forms a scab.

The scab falls off after the skin has healed.

What's a Bruise?

A bruise is a dark spot that appears after an injury. A blow to the body can cause **blood vessels** to break. This allows blood to collect under the skin, forming a bruise. A bruise may hurt when you touch it.

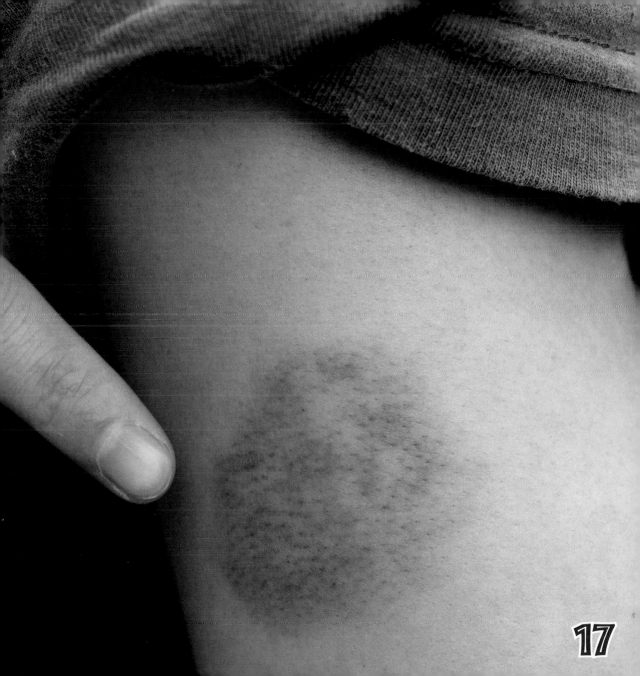

Black and Blue!

Bruises change color as they heal. At first, a bruise looks red from the blood. However, bruises quickly turn dark blue or purple. After a while, the bruise will fade. Then it may look green, yellow, or brown.

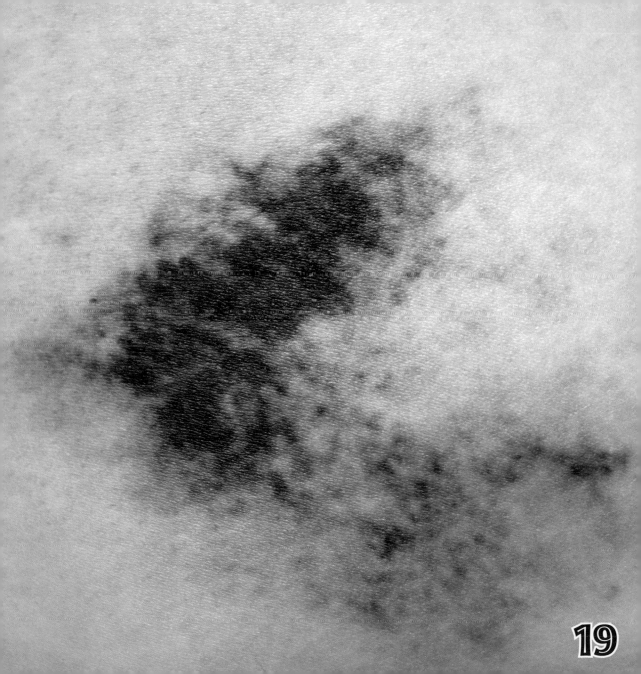

Caring for Bruises

Bruises don't usually need care. Putting ice on them right after an injury will help keep swelling down. You should see a doctor if you have a bruise that is hard, gets bigger, or doesn't go away after a few weeks.

Glossary

blood vessel: a small tube in a person's body that carries blood

clot: a lump made when something sticks together and gets thicker

germ: a tiny creature that can cause illness

scar: a mark left on the skin after an injury heals

stitch: a tiny knot used to sew cuts closed

wound: an injury caused by a cut or blow to the body

For More Information

Books

Landau, Elaine. *Bumps, Bruises, and Scrapes.* Tarrytown, NY: Marshall Cavendish Benchmark, 2009.

Lang, Elizabeth. *First Aid Basics.* Mankato, MN: Child's World, 2013.

Websites

Dealing with Cuts
kidshealth.org/parent/firstaid_safe/emergencies/bleeding.html#cat149
Find out how to care for cuts.

KidsHealth
kidshealth.org/kid
Read more about cuts, bruises, and many other health topics.

Index